WORKING STEAM
Collett & Hawksworth Halls

Roy Hobbs

Ian Allan
60th ANNIVERSARY

Introduction

The GWR 'Hall' class 4-6-0s represented one of the most numerous and successful mixed-traffic 4-6-0 designs operated by a pre-nationalisation company, their number only being exceeded by their equally well-known Class 5 cousins of the former LMS.

The operating departments of the GWR were, in the early 1920s, becoming concerned with shortcomings being experienced with the performance of the '43xx' class 2-6-0s. This had been noticed particularly with a fast express goods duty, comprising 50 covered vans, running between Southall and Wolverhampton. It was determined that the boiler was unable to meet the continuous demands placed upon it, as complaints of poor steaming were manifest, the situation being relieved only if a number of signal checks allowed rebuilding of the fire. All of this resulted in considerable work for the fireman.

The decision was taken to carry out a rebuild of 'Saint' class 4-6-0 No 2925 *Saint Martin* with smaller driving wheels of 6ft 0in diameter, to provide the prototype of a new mixed-traffic type with wide utilisation. This appeared in 1925, following which an extensive series of trials was carried out. This took place initially in the West Country when No 2925 was allocated to Laira shed, working mainly on passenger duties between Plymouth and Penzance, with occasional goods turns. During 1928 and 1929 the first production examples appeared, and, numbered in the '4900' series, were sent to the West Country to join *Saint Martin*, itself now renumbered 4900.

Between 1928 and 1943, in addition to the prototype, some 258 examples were built to Collett's original design, which were, with certain exceptions, named after stately homes.

By the mid-1930s examples of the class could be found widely across the system but especially on services in the county of Cornwall.

On Collett's retirement in 1941 he was succeeded by F. W. Hawksworth, who decided on some radical improvements to the general design. The basic Churchward arrangement, using bar frames at the front end, was abandoned in favour of plate frames throughout, together with a plate-framed bogie. At the same time, the standard No 1 boiler was adapted to include a large three-row superheater, providing a marked increase in the degree of superheat.

These modifications were found entirely successful, and the 'Modified Halls' ('6959' class) soon became equally popular with both shed and operating staff. Between 1944 and 1950 some 71 examples of the revised design were constructed, comprising Nos 6959-6999 and 7900-7929.

Apart from No 4911 *Bowden Hall,* condemned following a direct bomb hit at Keyham in 1941, the class remained intact until 1959 when the prototype, No 4900, was officially withdrawn. The last examples, Nos 6952 *Kimberley Hall* and 7925 *Westol Hall,* went at the end of WR steam operation in December 1965. Fortunately, several examples of both series have survived into preservation, due to the existence of the Barry locomotive graveyard.

In compiling this album, reference has been made to a number of sources, and *Great Western 4-6-0s at Work* (M. Rutherford) along with *The GWR Mixed Traffic 4-6-0 Classes* (O. S. Nock) have been particularly helpful in this respect. Magazines have included the *Great Western Railway Journal*, *Railway Magazine*, *Steam World*, *Trains Illustrated* and the RCTS *Railway Observer*. Finally, my grateful thanks must be given to several photographers for their assistance, but especially to Alan Jarvis, Trevor Owen and Dick Riley without whose help publication could not have been achieved.

Roy Hobbs
Exeter
May 2002

First published 2002

ISBN 0 7110 2903 2

All rights reserved. No part of this book may be reproduced or transmitted in any form or by any means, electronic or mechanical, including photo-copying, recording or by any information storage and retrieval system, without permission from the Publisher in writing.

© Roy Hobbs 2002

Published by Ian Allan Publishing

an imprint of Ian Allan Publishing Ltd, Hersham, Surrey KT12 4RG.
Printed by Ian Allan Printing Ltd, Hersham, Surrey KT12 4RG.

Code: 0209/B2

Title page: Featured at probably the most familiar railway location in Devon, No 4978 *Westwood Hall* is seen on 9 June 1962 heading a westbound holiday train at Shell Cove, near Dawlish. Withdrawn in September 1964, it received a final accolade that month, replacing failed diesel-hydraulic No D835 *Pegasus* at Castle Cary on the 9.20am Falmouth-Paddington service. *L. F. Folkard*

Below: In beautifully clean condition, No 4948 *Northwick Hall* stands at Newton Abbot (83A) depot on 19 July 1958. Reporting number 535 refers to the 1.40pm Kingswear-Paddington service. It was one of 11 of the type converted to burn oil in 1946/7, when it was renumbered 3902. The scheme was short-lived, and on re-conversion it reverted to its original identity. *R. C. Riley*

Above: Class prototype No 4900 *Saint Martin* is seen at Old Oak Common MPD (81A) in September 1956 with less than three years before withdrawal. It had by this time been further standardised following overhaul, and during 1948 was fitted with a new front end incorporating outside steam pipes. One driver considered it a free steamer and noted that, when worked hard, the cylinders appeared to 'rock back and forth in rhythm with the big ends'. *R. C. Riley*

Right: Close to the departure platforms of Paddington station, No 4962 *Ragley Hall* is observed marshalling a lengthy 2.20pm Paddington-Shrewsbury parcels working on 4 April 1957. The tender still bears the original design of BR crest, which was superseded in 1957. Official allocation at this time was to Reading (81D) depot, but a period in the 1960s was spent in the Neath division, before a final return to the London district. *R. C. Riley*

Above: The 3.55pm from Paddington linking London and South Wales, and named the 'Capitals United Express' in 1956, was first established between the wars. No 6991 *Acton Burnell Hall* is shown having cleared Westbourne Bridge, shortly after leaving the terminus with the down working on 13 July 1957. Westbourne Bridge was close by Ranelagh Bridge servicing point which, possessing a turntable, avoided the necessity for locomotives having to visit Old Oak Common depot before their return workings. *R. C. Riley*

Right: In a location close to that opposite, No 4949 *Packwood Hall* is shown with the 3.45pm Paddington-West Wales service on 27 August 1960. It was selected, along with 20 other class members, to employ the BR standard piston-valve head for comparison with the Western semi-plug design. After lengthy testing the experiment was concluded in May 1958. The prolonged trials required to resolve a high-frequency vibration problem, noted on some engines when coasting at speed, acted against their continuation. *R. C. Riley*

One of the class that featured in the BR 1948 Locomotive Exchanges, arranged to evaluate typical designs of the Big Four companies, is shown passing Old Oak Common on 19 October 1963 with a coal train for Kensal Green gasworks. No 6990 *Witherslack Hall* was employed on Eastern Region passenger duties between Marylebone and Manchester, to which route it was limited due to its width over cylinders. Partly the result of mechanical problems, plus over-cautious running, it failed to provide the performance experienced with the class on its home territory, the trial results proving disappointing. Although withdrawn in December 1965, it was rescued from Barry in 1975, and can now be seen at Loughborough (GCR), running over a section it previously covered in 1948. *T. B. Owen*

Towards the end of steam power on the Western Region most of the remaining locomotives took on a generally run-down appearance, often with nameplates and other identification removed, whilst normal locomotive cleaning effectively ended. In this view, taken during June 1965 in the last days of steam from Paddington, an unidentified 'Modified Hall' approaches Old Oak Common on the down relief line with what is probably a semi-fast working from the terminus during the late afternoon. *Roy Hobbs*

Below: In this interesting portrait taken at Old Oak Common depot (81A) on 5 May 1956, No 7903 *Foremarke Hall* has the initial lined-black livery used by BR for mixed-traffic types. This was replaced from 1956 when the class was painted in the lined Brunswick green used for the WR's main passenger classes. No 7903 is now at Blundson, near Swindon, undergoing restoration. *R. C. Riley*

Right: The second in the first production batch of the class, No 4902 *Aldenham Hall,* built in 1928, passes Hanwell & Elthorne station with an up express on 6 October 1958. A lady, meanwhile, attends to her infant charge in a vintage perambulator, oblivious to the train's roar. The smokebox paintwork suggests recent front-end attention, possibly at Swindon Works. *K. W. Wightman*

In this scene No 6985 *Parwick Hall* is observed close to Hayes & Harlington station on 27 April 1963, with a Wembley-bound special for the annual Schoolboys' International soccer tournament. During this yearly event WR locomotives, along with other 'foreign' engines, were stabled at Neasden depot. No 6985 was selected in 1953, along with nine other 'Modified Halls', to be fitted with a new chimney and blastpipe of revised proportions, following Swindon test plant experiments. The object was to improve boiler steaming capacity. Subsequent reports showed that, apart from 'a rather sharp blast on the fire on starting which reduced on notching up', pressure could be maintained for longer without blower use. The modification was made standard for AK-pattern boilers in July 1954. *Roy Denison*

In beautifully prepared condition, No 7900 *Saint Peter's Hall* heads towards London along the up relief line, near Twyford, with a lengthy parcels working on 19 April 1958. The wide variety of vans, including both bogie and four-wheeled stock, will be noted. After an early allocation to Bristol St Philips Marsh (82B), No 7900 spent the remainder of its working life at Oxford (81F) depot, presumably arising from its named association with the university city. *T. B. Owen*

Left: The final member of the class, No 7929 *Wyke Hall*, completed in November 1950, approaches Twyford station with a down express to Carmarthen on 27 July 1963. Swindon obviously took special care in its construction, as it was considered the best 'Modified Hall'. One outstanding journey was its employment on a 12-coach Birmingham to Weston-super-Mare excursion in the mid-1950s, when it completed the round trip of 350 miles on just one tender of coal. *R. C. Riley*

Above: No 5922 *Caxton Hall* is seen passing through Twyford station on 12 May 1959 with an early-morning up express working from Bristol. The DMU on the far platform is possibly from the Henley branch, the junction signals being just visible above the platform canopy on the right-hand side of the picture. No 5922 was involved in electric lighting experiments in 1949. Constructed in 1933 as part of Lot 281, it was condemned in January 1964. *T. B. Owen*

Left: Seen west of Twyford, No 6994 *Baggrave Hall* takes the down through line on 21 April 1956 with a westbound express working consisting of a rake of coaches in the carmine and cream livery used for main-line stock, until succeeded by either lined maroon livery or the original GWR colours of chocolate and cream on certain formations during the mid-1950s. No 6994 survived until November 1964, being condemned at Oxley (2B) depot. *T. B. Owen*

Above: A view taken near Sonning, with a rather untidy No 5907 *Marble Hall* in charge of an afternoon down semi-fast working on 8 August 1959. It is seen attached to one of the later pattern Hawksworth 4,000gal flush-sided tenders, these often being exchanged on periodic works visits. No 5907 was included in an early batch of class withdrawals, being taken out of service in November 1961 along with seven further examples that year. *K. W. Wightman*

Below: In a scene characterising the winter of 1963, No 5943 *Elmdon Hall* heads along the up relief line, near Sonning, with a parcels duty on 26 January. A Hawksworth 4,000-gallon tender is fitted, these being first introduced in October 1947 on No 6974. *T. B. Owen*

Right: In this beautiful back-lit study No 4956 *Plowden Hall* is shown approaching Twyford with an up boat train from Fishguard Harbour to Paddington on 5 December 1959. A Cardiff Canton (88A) engine at this time, it was later allocated to Westbury (82D) MPD. *T. B. Owen*

Left: In this view taken near Sonning No 5960 *Saint Edmund Hall* is depicted on 21 April 1956 with a down semi-fast duty similar to that illustrated earlier. The engine is a further example in the rather untidy condition typical of those used an lesser duties, mainly as a result of manpower shortages often caused by better-paid local employment then available. No 5960, as with No 7900, was almost continuously allocated to Oxford (81F) in BR days. *T. B. Owen*

Above: An eight-coach evening commuter working heads towards Reading, near Sonning, on 29 June 1961 in the charge of No 5956 *Horsley Hall.* On 14 August 1954, when heading the 7.35am Birkenhead to Margate working, this locomotive was diverted via Kensington Olympia. No SR engine being available, it continued forward to Redhill over the Brighton main line — a prohibited route! Impounded at Redhill, it was returned six days later. *T. B. Owen*

Below: One of the final batch of the 'Modified Hall' series built in November 1950 is seen here having passed through Twyford and heading towards Sonning with a down Class F mixed freight on 5 December 1959. No 7924 *Thornycroft Hall* was one of 10 engines chosen for chimney and blastpipe modifications on AK-pattern boilers in 1953, these later being adopted as standard. *T. B. Owen*

Right: Taking the up relief line in Sonning Cutting on 10 September 1960, another work-stained example of the class, No 4986 *Aston Hall,* heads a nine-coach stopping service. Built in 1931, it was included in the first significant batch of withdrawals during 1962, when 74 examples were condemned as a result of the dieselisation of the work for which they had been responsible. *K. W. Wightman*

Left: In Sonning Cutting, a favourite photographic location over the years, No 6949 *Haberfield Hall* is depicted with an ECS working towards London on 2 May 1959 whilst a ganger patiently awaits its passing. This engine was involved in the disastrous Baschurch accident of 13 February 1961, when the 6.37pm Wellington-Chester express ran into the leading bogie bolster wagon of the 6.25pm Coton Hill-Saltley unfitted freight, which had failed to clear the main line during a shunting movement. Regrettably, both driver and fireman failed to survive the accident, along with two other railway staff. The cause was partly attributed to lack of suitable track circuiting, which would have eliminated clearance of the section for the express. This was installed at Baschurch shortly after. The severe damage sustained by No 6949 resulted in its official withdrawal in May 1961. *T. B. Owen*

Right: Taking the West of England route at Southcote Junction on 4 July 1959, No 4987 *Brockley Hall* is seen heading an unidentified local working, probably from Paddington to Newbury. During 1954 this locomotive was selected for an experiment which involved replacing the conventional firebox brick arch with one of concrete. This became unserviceable after little more than a week and was replaced by the standard arch. A similar trial on '43xx' class 2-6-0 No 9319 was equally unsuccessful, being discontinued after around two months. As normal brick arch life averaged about four months, the experiments were abandoned. No 4987 was also involved in the piston valve investigations mentioned earlier. Operating life was spent mainly in the London Division during the 1950s, a late location being Southall (81C) MPD.
R. C. Riley

Above: The platforms at Basingstoke station can just be discerned in the distance as No 5901 *Hazel Hall* heads a Class E freight towards Reading on 2 March 1957. The BRITISH RAILWAYS legend on the tender in GWR style was introduced immediately following nationalisation. *K. W. Wightman*

Right: The GWR and subsequently WR had running powers over SR metals from Basingstoke to such destinations as Southampton and Bournemouth, several through passenger workings taking place. In this view No 6913 *Levens Hall* leaves with what is possibly a through service to the North via Oxford in the late 1950s. *K. W. Wightman*

No 7927 *Willington Hall* is shown on Southern Region territory at Southampton Terminus, whilst backing on to its train on 26 June 1957. This is probably a local service to Reading. The locomotive is in the first BR mixed-traffic livery of black with red lining, which was later replaced by GWR-style lined Brunswick green, starting with No 6997 *Bryn-Ivor Hall* from 1956 onwards. No 7927 lasted until the end of Western Region steam operation in December 1965 and was allocated to Oxford (81F) at the time of withdrawal. It was subsequently sent to Woodham Bros at Barry Dock, but like other examples was eventually rescued for preservation. *R. C. Riley*

Several Western Region branches under threat of closure were visited by organised railtours prior to the event. Here No 6963 *Throwley Hall* expends maximum effort as it tackles the steep climb on the approach to Devizes. This came shortly after leaving the branch junction at Patney & Chirton whilst heading the LCGB 'Wessex Downsman' of 4 April 1965 on its way from Reading to Bath. Until the direct line via Westbury was opened in 1900, the branch enjoyed secondary main-line status for trains to the West of England. However, it succumbed to the Beeching closure programme in April 1966, when it was shut to all traffic. Built in 1944, No 6963 spent its time in the early 1950s in the Shrewsbury district, but was latterly a London Division engine until withdrawal took place some three months after this working, in July 1965. *Roy Hobbs*

Left: At the lonely outpost of Holt Junction, between Chippenham and Westbury, No 7928 *Wolf Hall*, built in November 1950 and the penultimate member of the class, makes its way south with a short Class K freight on 14 July 1962. The line to Devizes opened from Holt Junction in July 1857, and can be seen diverging behind the signalbox. From construction No 7928 was always based at Worcester (85A) MPD until withdrawal in March 1965. *Roy Denison*

Above: Wellington Bank, east of Whiteball Tunnel in Somerset, will always be associated with the 102mph run of 'City' class 4-4-0 *City of Truro* when heading an up 'Ocean Mails' express in 1904. No 5967 *Bickmarsh Hall* is seen on 17 June 1958, having left the summit by the tunnel's western entrance with a down Class E freight. Removed from Barry scrapyard in 1987, it now awaits restoration on the Pontypool & Blaenavon Railway. *T. B. Owen*

Shortly after arrival at the now demolished Tiverton Junction station, No 4904 *Binnegar Hall* is seen with an up local service, probably in the summer of 1962. The Hemyock branch train, headed by '14xx' class 0-4-2T No 1451, is visible on the left-hand side, whilst sister engine No 1471 waits opposite, probably with the Tiverton connection. Marking the 1904 record of *City of Truro* along this route,

'Castle' class 4-6-0 No 4079 *Pendennis Castle* headed a commemorative railtour on 5 May 1964. Unfortunately, it failed at Westbury, being replaced by an unprepared No 6999 *Capel Dewi Hall*. However, on its run to Taunton, 86½mph was attained near Langport, the highest recorded with the type. No 4904, one of five 'Halls' built in 1928, was condemned in December 1963. *L. F.Folkard*

Cowley Bridge Junction is where the lines of the former GWR merged with those of the SR from Plymouth via Okehampton. No 6995 *Benthall Hall* passes with the 4.50pm from Taunton to Exeter St Davids on 5 July 1961. The locomotive participated in Royal Train duties in May 1964, when it double-headed with 'Castle' No 5071 *Spitfire* on the short section between Torquay and Aller Junction. *R. C. Riley*

Below: An unusual view of No 4993 *Dalton Hall* marshalling the ECS of the 6.20pm from Taunton in the late afternoon of 23 June 1962. Exeter St Davids station is around a mile from the city centre, Exeter Central on the Southern route being much closer. The background houses give an indication of the gradient between them, and why banking was often necessary. *R. C. Riley*

Right: In a further view taken at Exeter St Davids No 4905 *Barton Hall* is seen departing with a westbound parcels train in July 1963. This engine was the first of the class to employ a mechanical lubricator in the postwar period, this being fitted in 1947. Initial trials were carried out in 1931/2 on Nos 4941 *Llangedwyn Hall* and No 4950 *Patshull Hall*, but these were not developed. *T. B. Owen*

During the changeover from steam to diesel traction, the two forms of motive power could often be found in tandem, sometimes with a steam locomotive assisting a failed example of its modern counterpart. In this scene No 6965 *Thirlestaine Hall* is piloting 'Warship' class No D802 *Formidable* at the well-known location of Shell Cove, near Dawlish, a favourite of the GWR Publicity Department. The train is an unidentified down express, photographed on 9 June 1962. No 6965 was one of 55 class members that were unnamed when first built but which eventually received their nameplates between 1946 and 1948. In the interim, the lettering HALL CLASS was painted below the centre splasher beading. The reason behind the original action was stated to be the shortage of brass during World War 2, when these engines were placed into service. *L. F. Folkard*

Seen here alongside the sea wall near Teignmouth, No 4992 *Crosby Hall* heads an up stopping service, the 9.20am from Kingswear to Exeter St Davids, on 18 July 1958. This scene holds special memories for me as, some 11 years previously, I had the privilege when a young schoolboy of enjoying my first illicit main-line trip along this stretch of line on a similar train hauled by No 4988 *Bulwell Hall*. Another young friend, with a driver relative, organised this trip for us between Teignmouth and Exeter St Thomas, which still remains an unforgettable experience! No 4992 was to continue in service until officially condemned in April 1965. *R. C. Riley*

Illustrated on the approach to Teignmouth station, No 4955 *Plaspower Hall* is shown with an unidentified westbound working in June 1960. The coastal section between here and Dawlish Warren is noted for its instability, suffering from severe erosion due to wave action, particularly during winter storms. This often results in only the up line being available for traffic. *Geoff Rixon*

Running over a section of what is now the Torbay & Dartmouth Steam Railway from Paignton to Kingswear, No 6938 *Corndean Hall* leaves Goodrington Sands Halt with a down stopping service on a rather grey day during the summer of 1961. The line was taken over for private operation following closure by BR in 1973. No 6938 was transferred from Newton Abbot district to the London Division following area dieselisation, being operated by Reading (81D) depot on withdrawal in March 1965. *L. F. Folkard*

Left: Aller Junction is the point, west of Newton Abbot, at which the respective lines to Torbay and Plymouth diverge, and the start of the severe two-mile climb to Dainton summit. No 4975 *Umberslade Hall* is seen at Langford's Bridge on 28 June 1961 with duty Z10, the return Buckfastleigh Sunday Schools' annual excursion from Teignmouth. What is probably a '28xx' class 2-8-0 can be seen occupying the goods loop, with an NBL 'D63xx' class diesel banker at the rear. The Torbay route to Kingswear can be discerned by the line of telegraph poles above the end of the train. *L. F. Folkard*

Above: On one of the steeper stretches of line between Newton Abbot and Dainton Summit at Stoneycombe siding, No 6936 *Breccles Hall* heads a down express on 17 June 1958. The line rises here at 1 in 41 for around ⅛ mile, steepening to 1 in 36 before Dainton Tunnel. By the summer of 1964 diesel traction was virtually in complete charge of the section west of Exeter, and just six steam diagrams remained. However, on 24 June No 6936 replaced a failed diesel at Exeter, on the Plymouth section of the 1pm from Waterloo, shortly before its own withdrawal that November. *T. B. Owen*

Below: Tackling another of the severe climbs on the main route to Plymouth, No 7907 *Hart Hall* heads an unidentified express near Tigley on 22 July 1961. The train is ascending Rattery Bank, between Totnes and Brent, which includes a half mile section of 1 in 52 and one as steep as 1 in 46. No 7907 spent its working life in the Bristol area before withdrawal in December 1965. *T. B. Owen*

Right: Ivybridge was among several intermediate stations between Plymouth and Newton Abbot which closed during March 1959, due to the planned withdrawal of certain main-line stopping services. However, due to population growth, a new station opened on a different site in July 1994. No 5945 *Leckhampton Hall* passes the original structure on 14 June 1958 with a down train. *L. F. Folkard*

Left: The first obstacle for eastbound trains leaving Plymouth is Hemerdon Bank, between Plympton and Ivybridge. Rising at 1 in 42 for around 1¹/₂ miles, it here proves a challenge for No 6988 *Swithland Hall* as it pilots No 4090 *Dorchester Castle* with an unidentified train on 14 June 1958. Mainly a Bristol Division engine, No 6988's first depot was Weymouth (82F) through the early 1950s, with later transfers to Bristol Bath Road (82A), Plymouth Laira (83D) and Westbury (82D), before withdrawal in September 1964. *T. B. Owen*

Above: Amidst scenery typical of the main line through Cornwall, No 4908 *Broome Hall* crosses one of its many picturesque viaducts with an eastbound stopping service on 13 September 1958. It is shown tackling the more than six-mile climb to Doublebois from Bodmin Road with its ruling 1 in 70 gradient. St Pinnock Viaduct, shown here, was the tallest among no fewer than 31 of these structures situated on the section between Truro and Saltash. *T. B. Owen*

Above: Shown a little way west of the previous location, No 6911 *Holker Hall* is illustrated in charge of an up working to Sheffield, shortly after having passed Bodmin Road station on 26 July 1958. The line between Saltash and Truro is extremely testing with many severe curves and gradients. Authority O. S. Nock considered the Collett version equal to the 'Castle' class on this route with superior hill-climbing ability. *T. B. Owen*

Right: Passing over Goring troughs, No 4937 *Lanelay Hall* is heading a Class H freight consisting largely of wooden-bodied coal wagons, on 27 February 1960. Prior to its 1962 withdrawal it was based at Pontypool Road (86G) depot, and a typical two-day freight duty could have been outward to Shrewsbury with a Margam-Saltney working, then continuing on a local duty to Saltney and returning home next day with an early-morning trip from this point. *T. B. Owen*

Left: Possibly not long after a visit to Swindon Works, No 6982 *Melmerby Hall* is seen at Goring with an up local passenger working consisting of just two coaches, on 4 November 1961. This could have been a running-in turn, as stopping services between Swindon and Reading were often used for this purpose. No 6982 spent its entire working life in the Bristol Division following construction in January 1948 until withdrawal in August 1964. *T. B. Owen*

Above: The penultimate engine of Collett's original design, No 6957 *Norcliffe Hall*, passes Uffington between Swindon and Didcot with an up parcels working on 26 April 1959. During April 1947 it was one of 11 class members converted for oil burning, under a plan initiated in 1946, and renumbered 3952. This short-lived scheme arose originally from coal supply problems. Some 84 'Halls' were to be modified, but the plan was abandoned in 1948. *T. B. Owen*

In the usual resplendent condition which followed overhaul at Swindon, No 4917 *Crosswood Hall* is seen here in the works yard on 15 March 1958. During this period it was based at Westbury (82D) depot, where it would have been mainly employed on freight duties. However, from 1947 one of the depot's engines, No 6978 *Haroldstone Hall*, was allocated to its small former GWR sub-shed at Salisbury (SAL). This was specially retained to work one passenger diagram, the 11.17am Salisbury-Cardiff and 4.35pm return. For this duty it was always maintained in exemplary order. Following closure of the shed in 1950, servicing was transferred to the Southern Region depot, where interest declined, with no special engine being subsequently allocated. *T. B. Owen*

Passing through the Cotswold junction of Kemble on the route between Gloucester and Swindon, No 4941 *Llangedwyn Hall* heads an up express in the London direction during September 1960.

Along with No 4950 *Patshull Hall*, it was fitted with a mechanical lubrication system in the early 1930s. This equipment was not made standard until 1950, starting with No 7910 *Hown Hall*. *Alan Jarvis*

A view here between Cheltenham and Gloucester, with No 7918 *Rhose Wood Hall* heading west through Churchdown with a Class H mixed freight on 5 June 1962. A typical Monday-Friday freight duty for this Tyseley (84E) engine in the summer 1963 timetable would have been Diagram TYS403, commencing with the 12.25pm Washwood Heath-Stoke Gifford, then continuing the next day on the 1.30am Bristol-Severn Tunnel Junction and proceeding to Margam, finally returning on the third day to Bordesley Junction with the 9.55pm from Margam. No 7918 was withdrawn in February 1965. *Alan Jarvis*

No 5975 *Winslow Hall* of St Philips Marsh (82B) depot, passes Bristol Temple Meads station on 27 March 1962 with a Class C working. The 1963 Through Freight Index showed the type still active from Bristol, with trips to the Birmingham/Wolverhampton area, Chester and to Woodford Halse (GCR). The latter destination was part of Diagram BL403, the 7.50pm Severn Beach-Woodford (WO for York), returning SO Woodford-Severn Beach with the 4.50am from York.
Alan Jarvis

Left: Soon after leaving Bristol Temple Meads No 7907 *Hart Hall* slowly eases its Class E freight past Bedminster on 19 October 1963. It is fitting to mention here a sensational run by No 7904 *Fountains Hall* in September 1954. Replacing a defective 'Castle' on the up 'Bristolian' at Little Somerford, it averaged 82mph. over some 75 miles, a maximum of 84mph being recorded at Pangbourne. Despite the delay it was only 15min late on arrival, *eight* minutes being cut from the Swindon to Paddington schedule. *John Wiltshire*

Above: The North & West route from Newport via Hereford and Shrewsbury was well used by both passenger and especially freight traffic. No 7926 *Willey Hall* gets under way from Newport with the 8.50am (SO) to Newcastle on 4 August 1962. It will soon face two difficult climbs, first to Pontypool Road and then a four-mile rise, mostly at 1 in 82, from Abergavenny to Llanvihangel. Here a banking engine was provided to give assistance, where necessary, to freight workings. No 7926 was withdrawn in December 1964. *John Wiltshire*

As No 6958 *Oxburgh Hall* waits in the up through road with a short ECS train, No 6915 *Mursley Hall* departs Newport High Street with an express duty on 12 July 1960. A point of note with No 6915 is the silvered buffers, suggesting a previous special working. No 6958, the final example of Collett's original 'Hall' series, is seen to be fitted with an AK-pattern boiler incorporating a three-row superheater and new-style capuchonless chimney providing improved steaming characteristics. Both engines, however, bear the the 'X' cabside marking, first introduced in wartime to show engines in good mechanical condition that were capable of hauling trains beyond the normally permitted load. No 6915 survived until February 1965, with No 6958 being condemned the following June. *John Edgington*

Shortly after leaving Newport Tunnel, and against the town's suburban background, No 5990 *Dorford Hall* is seen heading westwards in the Cardiff direction with a down express working, duty F19, on 27 July 1963. No 5990 was amongst 21 of the class used for the piston valve experiments mentioned previously and which were abandoned in 1958. During the 1960s it was a Banbury (84C) engine and would have been much involved with freight duties from this depot. Regular trips took Banbury's allocation to London, Westbury and Bristol alongside work within the Wolverhampton Division. One typical two-day cycle involved the 9pm Banbury-Greenford, the 1.22am Park Royal-Bordesley Junction and return, whilst another one-day duty covered the 5.25pm Banbury-Stoke Gifford, returning home with the 10.15pm from Bristol, both of these being weekday workings.

John Wiltshire

Below: Heading a Portsmouth express, No 6909 *Frewin Hall* is seen approaching Marshfield on 30 June 1962. A 1954 experiment with chrome-plated valve liners was halted in 1956, due mainly to the excessive ring wear experienced. *John Wiltshire*

Right: In a further scene taken close to Marshfield, a rather untidy No 5961 *Toynbee Hall* was in charge of a down express on 13 July 1963. Latterly a Neath Division engine, it was withdrawn in August 1965. *Alan Jarvis*

Left: As '94xx' 0-6-0PT No 8446 sets off from Cardiff (Pengam) yard with a brake van, No 4908 *Broome Hall*, illustrated previously in Cornwall, heads a short Class C freight towards the city on 8 August 1962. Following an extended stay at Penzance (83G) depot in the late 1950s, it migrated to the London Division and was officially allocated to both Reading (81D) and Didcot (81E) depots towards the end of its working life. Its rather careworn appearance indicates likely involvement in freight duties over a lengthy period. *John Wiltshire*

Above: Passing Newtown West signalbox in Cardiff, No 4936 *Kinlet Hall* is observed on 11 June 1963 in charge of another short westbound freight. During 1953 it was selected for trials comparing manganese steel with bronze liners then used in coupled axleboxes. Though wear figures were excellent, manpower problems involved in further conversions resulted in scheme abandonment in 1963. Sold in January 1964 to Woodham's of Barry, No 4936 was privately purchased in May 1981 and has been restored to GWR livery. *Alan Jarvis*

Above: The Cardiff-Portsmouth service was one of the first inter-company workings, being introduced in 1896. There were latterly five trains each way weekdays in steam days, with two on Sundays. 'Halls' were the regular GWR motive power, with rolling stock being provided by both SR and GWR, and later each region. No 6918 *Sandon Hall* is seen near Rumney River Bridge on 23 April 1963, passing one of South Wales' numerous coal trains with the 10.30am from Cardiff. *Alan Jarvis*

Right: Whilst young train spotters eagerly add to their 'ABC' entries and a '72xx' class 2-8-2T passes with an oil tank train, No 6908 *Downham Hall* waits at Cardiff General to move the empty stock from another Portsmouth working on 6 April 1963. Its life in the postwar era was spent in the Bristol Division, mainly at St Philips Marsh (82B) depot, the locomotive being withdrawn in July 1965 from Barrow Road (82E). *Alan Jarvis*

Under the observant eye of a local watchman, No 5904 *Kelham Hall*, in presentable external condition, berths the Southern Region stock of a Portsmouth-Cardiff working in the local Canton carriage sidings on 10 June 1963. Of note is the unique Collett 4,000 gallon eight-wheeled tender fitted to No 5904 at this time. Predominantly a Bristol Division engine from the middle 1950s, it had spent some years in the early BR era based at Oxford (81F) depot. During this time it would have been occupied mainly with passenger work. At Oxford, two of the class in best condition were allocated as station pilots and also for standby passenger duties. Freight work around this period included trips to Oxley and to Birmingham (Bordesley Junction) as well as a parcels duty to Crewe. *Alan Jarvis*

Barry Island was, and still is, a popular South Wales seaside resort, and throughout the 1950s and 1960s special trains operated from all parts of the WR, as well as further afield, and converged on its station.

No 5983 *Henley Hall* heads an excursion from Tyseley at Grangetown on 5 August 1962. Based at Southall (81C) in the 1950s, it ended its days at Tyseley (2A) in April 1965. *Alan Jarvis*

Left: In this view No 6993 *Arthog Hall* is shown passing Cogan Junction with a special from Cheltenham for Barry Island on 5 August 1963. Here the metals of the Barry Railway separated from those of the Taff Vale system. Having been allocated in its early years to Weymouth (82F), where it would have worked the Channel Island boat trains, it then moved to the Worcester Division before condemnation at Oxford (81F) in December 1965. *John Wiltshire*

Above: Another Barry Island excursion, this time with an unidentified 'Modified Hall' heading a train from Leicester past Cogan on 12 August 1962. The success of the 'Modified Halls' lay particularly in the boiler design, with its much increased degree of superheat. On their introduction they were used along with 'Castles' on the Bristol-Paddington services, recorders stating that it was often difficult to detect any marked differences in performance. *Alan Jarvis*

Running parallel with the main A473 road between Llantrisant and Bridgend, No 6987 *Shervington Hall* approaches the summit of the line at Llanharan with a Cardiff-Swansea working on 29 July 1963. It is also close to the junction of the former GWR line to Pyle via Tondu, which trailed in from a northwesterly direction. No 6987 was, at this period, based at Cardiff East Dock (88A) depot and would have been involved with its various freight turns. Regular goods workings would have taken it to Chester and the Birmingham/Wolverhampton locality. A typical 1963 diagram would have been duty CED400, which on weekdays involved the 1.10pm Cardiff-Saltney working, returning home from Chester with a freight commencing as the 7.55pm Edge Hill (Liverpool). No 6987, built 1948, survived until September 1964, during which year some 78 class members were condemned.
John Wiltshire

Tilehurst, just north of Reading, was situated on the line from Bristol to South Wales, which also afforded an alternative route to Birmingham via Didcot. No 6912 *Helmster Hall* is depicted in charge of a down express, hauling a rake of coaches painted in the chocolate and cream livery of the old company. The photograph was probably taken in the late 1950s. *K. W. Wightman*

Above: Newbury races produced considerable traffic and Newbury Racecourse station was provided to accommodate it. Paddington operated up to five non-stop workings on race days, whilst others originated from Oxford, Cardiff and Taunton. No 4918 *Dartington Hall* heads one such special near Hinksey South on 15 August 1959.

Right: Framed by an interesting selection of lower-quadrant signals, a splendidly prepared No 4956 *Plowden Hall* waits at Oxford on 15 August 1959 with the 7.10am Paddington-Wolverhampton service. The engine, which was to be withdrawn in July 1963, later returned on the 2.35pm Wolverhampton-Paddington service. *Both: R. C. Riley*

Left: Whilst the complete class had been officially withdrawn by December 1965, the final working of a scheduled WR steam-hauled train came on 3 January 1966, when the 10.30am Bournemouth-York service was taken forward from Oxford by No 6998 *Burton Agnes Hall*, now preserved. Latterly a London Division engine, it had spent periods at Cardiff Canton (86C) and Shrewsbury (84G) depots during the 1950s. On withdrawal it was bought direct from BR and is sometimes used on excursions from its Didcot base. *Roy Denison*

Above: Aynho Junction, near Banbury, was the location at which the GWR direct route from London to Birmingham joined that via Reading and Didcot. The former route, known as the Aynho cut-off, was an extension of the GWR/GCR joint route from Ashendon Junction. No 4966 *Shakenhurst Hall* is seen with the 8.55am Sheffield-Bournemouth train on 7 July 1962. The 'Halls' were regularly rostered on these summer cross-country through and relief workings to South Coast destinations. *T. B. Owen*

Recorded at Aynho Junction on 7 July 1962, No 6970 *Whaddon Hall* is seen in charge of the 10am Bradford Exchange-Poole holiday train, via Oxford and Reading. In postwar years two further unauthorised cross-country workings by the class were reported, similar to the Redhill incident mentioned earlier, and in each case beyond Nottingham. One of these involved No 6979 *Helperly Hall,* which reached York on 22 August 1959 with the 11.16am Bournemouth West-Newcastle service and returned two days later on the 5.30am York (Dringhouses)-Cardiff freight. The second concerned No 7912 *Little Linford Hall,* which arrived in Sheffield on 12 March 1964 with a Bournemouth-York train. Both, no doubt, again due to the lack of a replacement engine. *T. B. Owen*

Standing at Stourbridge Junction, the starting point for the Stourbridge Town branch, No 6922 *Burton Hall* is seen with a local service, probably that between Wolverhampton and Worcester, on 17 April 1964. Judging by its capuchonless chimney and the 'X' cabside marking, it now has the AK-type boiler fitted as standard on the 'Modified Hall' series. *Roy Denison*

In a view taken in the murky depths of the original Birmingham Snow Hill station, No 6942 *Eshton Hall* is shown waiting with an unidentified southbound express in 1963. The leading vehicle would appear to be of LNER Thompson design, so this could possibly be a regular summer timetable working from Newcastle to the South Coast. The station was totally demolished in the 1970s, but a completely new station on the site was opened in October 1987 for local commuter services and, from 1999, the Midland Metro light rail system. The latter now occupies much of the original formation via Wednesbury to Wolverhampton. *John Edgington*

In a further view taken in the vicinity of Birmingham Snow Hill, No 6983 *Otterington Hall* is seen approaching the station with the 1pm Shrewsbury-West London parcels working on 1 November 1955. The engine is painted in the initial BR mixed-traffic livery, whilst an even earlier 'GW' monogram surrounding the company coat-of-arms is still faintly evident on the locomotive's tender, despite the passing of nearly eight years since nationalisation. *John Edgington*

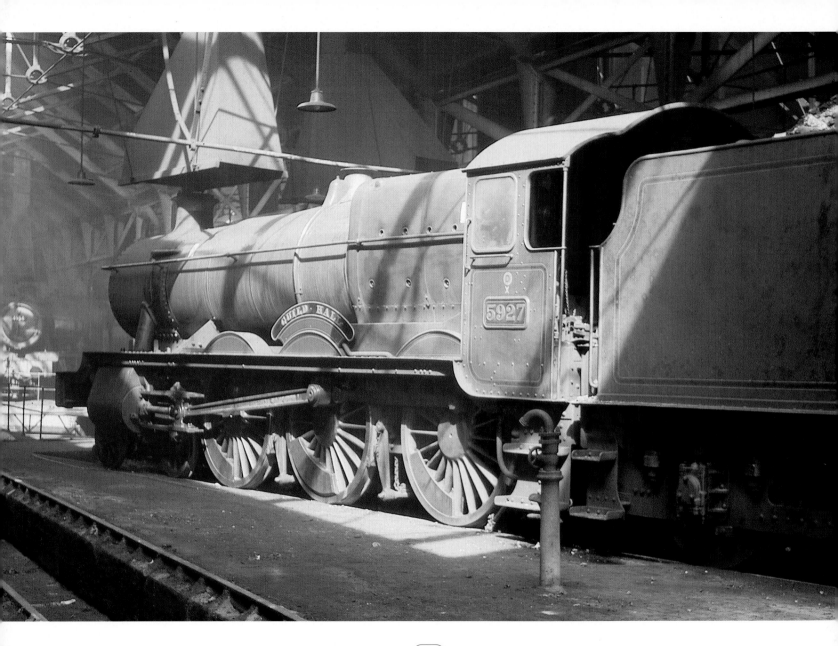

Left: Attracting a few shafts of sunlight, No 5927 *Guild Hall* is depicted at Oxley (84B) depot roundhouse on 1 April 1962. No 5927 was called upon for Royal duty in March 1954, when it relieved No 6028 *King George VI* at Hatton South Junction, taking Princess Margaret's train forward for stabling on the Alcester branch. It had an especially good reputation with engine crews, being an excellent steamer, in contrast to No 5936 *Oakley Hall*, which some drivers considered 'couldn't even steam standing still!'. *Geoff Rixon*

Above: A number of the class were fortunate enough to enter the ranks of preserved locomotives, due to the prolonged existence of Barry scrapyard, and 11 of the original series plus seven Hawksworth examples were saved. Two operating examples, Nos 4936 *Kinlet Hall* and 4965 *Rood Ashton Hall*, are seen near North Acton with an excursion from Kidderminster on 3 March 2001. Latterly known as No 4983, it was found that No 4965 had exchanged identity with this engine at Swindon in 1962 (although then unrecorded). *David Clark*

Index of Locations

Front cover: Passing Twyford East box and about to enter Twyford station with a down express working, No 6961 *Stedham Hall* is depicted with a mixed rake of coaching stock on 20 June 1959. Following representations to the BR Board, it was chosen for a comparative series of trials in late 1948, due to the unsatisfactory results obtained with No 6990 in the original BR 1948 Exchanges. These were extremely successful, with excellent power output and significantly lower consumption figures recorded. *T. B. Owen*

Rear cover: Shown entering the cutting on the approach to Reading West station, No 5963 *Wimpole Hall* heads an up stopping service on 2 May 1959. It has just cleared Southcote Junction, where the lines to Basingstoke and the West of England, via Newbury, separate. *T. B. Owen*

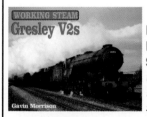